CLOUD COMPUTING PRIMER

Part One

Infinity to Beyond

BRIAN JOSEPH TURNER

First Published by: KES

82 London Road

Croydon

London

CR0 2TB

www.cloud-broker-online.com

ISBN: 978-1-47-529528-3

Date of Publication: April 2012

Dedicated to mum (Edna May Turner) whose inspiration gave me the courage to believe in myself and embark on the journey. To my wife and her continued support in all my endeavours. Without the encouragement this piece of work would not have been possible.

"If you have faith as much as a mustard seed you can move mountains"!

Contents

Introduction

Cloud Computing is defined as the emergence of the computing paradigm which makes data and services available from scalable data centres that can be accessed by any device that is connected via the internet. It leverages existing technology the internet, grid computing, Service Orientated Architecture and web services. It is a service that is subscribed to on a pay per use billing structure. It presents an opportunity for companies to control costs and manage shrinking IT budgets. In light of companies being required to become more efficient, reduce costs and collaborate globally. Cloud computing offers companies elasticity that enables organisation to grow or shrink their computing resources as needs dictate simplifying deployment and reducing the time to market. Organisations can take advantage of lower costs that are a direct result of cloud computing implementations. This allows the companies to take greater control of their capital expenditure (CAPEX).

1.0 Chapter One – To Infinity and Beyond

1.1 Technology Geared for Change

This section discusses the main business drivers the changing business environment, what cloud technology is used for and how cloud services are currently being used by both business and individuals to collaborate.

The current business environment is being influenced and shaped by three main drivers, knowledge, globalization and collaboration with each being enhanced and enabled by developments in Information Communications Technology; such as the internet, mobile and satellite communications. This has contributed to the digital economy which is characterised by use of ICT to undertake business processes. (Grant, 2010)

Cloud computing refers to scalable computing resources delivered as a service to your organisation as a metered service (you only pay for what you use). It represents a paradigm shift in how computer applications and infrastructures are accessed and implemented. All companies will be forced to compete on ideas as opposed to the IT resources at their disposal. Cloud Services now offer entrepreneurs the ability to build reliable and scalable solutions by using the virtual environments at fraction of a cost of the conventional application-hosting platforms (Turner, 2011). It is as simple as opening an account with Amazon, Google or Microsoft. Then you can start to build or deploy applications into the cloud. (Winans, et al, 2010)

Traditional desktops allow you run the applications locally on the PC or from a network server within a LAN or WAN topology. Cloud computing applications are stored on a server in a data centre that you access via an internet browser. The same principal applies to documents that you create as they are stored on a number of servers that can be accessed via an internet browser connection from anywhere in the world. For example, Google docs, Linkedin or drop box. If a user has the appropriate rights to the documents then they can access them on any device as long as they have an internet connection. (Miller, 2008)

We will now explore how the underlying technology is used to provide a cloud service.

Cloud computing provides users and or organisations access to enterprise class computing resources that were once the preserve of large multinationals and corporate with large cash reserves. This development has taken place due to the advent of the internet. With the desktop browser being the primary method of connecting to an infinite number of software applications that you or your organisation subscribe to. These individual services are brought together to develop services that merge to make a virtual network of IP addresses that exist in Cloud. This method of building applications allows you to access resources whether that is applications or infrastructure resources. This offers both SME's and corporates a distinct benefit through cost savings as they are no longer required to buy concurrent user licenses to access applications indefinitely they only pay for what they use similar to charging an oyster card or a mobile top up the difference being you pay after you have used the service. It has been found that collaborative applications are frequently used to facilitate global projects

with geographically dispersed teams. Some of the most well known collaborative tools on the market today are delivered as Software as a Service. These have now become household brands such as Google Apps, Facebook and Linkedin, for example these are social media sites that allow you to post your details on servers through applications that you would never need to buy a license to use or servers you will never own or physically have access to. This is a distinct difference from how we have traditionally consumed or managed ICT.

The following sub section outlines the transition from on premise systems to utility based model of cloud computing.

In this section the major issues are reviewed and discussed to discover how cloud computing became prevalent and how the first model of Infrastructure as a Service was developed and subsequently offered as service. The relevance and need for governance for both SME's and large corporate. The external drivers such as the global downturn and the drive to achieve operational efficiencies through the adoption of cloud computing.

Due to the growth of the internet and a need for collaborative projects across geographical boundaries and underutilised redundant server farms; Amazon decided to reuse some of their existing infrastructure (server farms) which they already used to power their search engine. These underutilised server farms were then used to power a new tranche of web enabled services. It provided a new tier of internet based group collaboration applications. (Miller, 2008)

Due to the major development of cloud computing there is a responsibility for management to understand the significance of this paradigm shift and where possible harness the technology to produce operational efficiencies and cost savings by implementing cloud services. As cited by (Winans, et al, 2010) that simply scaling your IT infrastructure does not mean that your systems will meet 21st century computing requirements. He alludes to something more than the technology, the need for an IT strategy that aligns and supports the core objectives of the business.

Globalization, economic crises, technology innovations and many other factors make it vital for businesses to develop and evolve away from current technical capabilities towards new architectures. (Winans, et al, 2010) In the face of global recession and retrenchment more companies are operating with skeleton staff with IT outsourcing becoming the norm. Therefore there is an emphasis on reducing capital expenditure and operational costs whilst maintaining organisational efficiency both at the local and global level. As such organisations are required to be agile and collaborate to achieve competitive advantage and market share. (De Silva, 2010) Cited, that companies that were disciplined in their implementation of cloud services managed to reduce their IT budget by 18% whilst their data centre costs were reduced by 16%. Why, because typically the implementation time and costs are reduced from weeks to days, even hours, and it reduces the total cost of ownership as there is no need to buy expensive hardware.

Therefore the potential of cloud computing is not limited to hosting applications in someone else's data centre (Turner, 2011). It is much more, it is the ability to elastically manage computing resources as seasonal demands or project needs dictate whilst removing the need to buy new infrastructure or to retain a large IT department. (Winans, et al, 2010)

(Winans, et al, 2010) Observations state that, cloud computing can be used to address tactical issues that organisations have to face in the areas of resource management, data centre management, operational standards and scalability. This viewpoint has merit as IT managers will testify operational standards and scalability are always issues that are at the top of the IT managers to do list. Therefore to realise these objectives are justification in itself for organisations to adopt cloud computing capabilities. (Turner, 2011) Not to mention the promise of being truly agile with the ability to collaborate with partners whilst benefiting from operational efficiencies and secure scalable solutions.

In this section we reviewed the external and contributory factors to organisations adopting the cloud, the potential of cloud computing and reasons for the adoption.

1.4 The Cloud Services Landscape

In this section we review the different types of cloud services and companies vying for market share in this new market. The list is not exhaustive however it does provide an overview of the type of services that are currently available.

1.4.1 Software as a Service (SaaS)

SaaS is software managed and distributed as a service; it offers purpose built business applications. In its most simplest form it is an application that is hosted by a service provider and delivered as a service to the customer on a pay per use basis via a web browser. It is a collection of scalable enterprise applications that have been designed to support a number of different customer requirements. The reason why this approach is attractive to the customer is that it does not require an upfront payment or the dedicated resources to perform a software development or deployment function. SaaS, at the time of writing is the most mature service offering of cloud computing services. This growth has been fuelled by Customer Relationship Management (CRM) systems of which Salesforce.com is at the forefront. It can also be concluded that a SaaS implementation has a lower market entry cost.

SaaS can be defined into two sub categories;

1. Packaged Software

Packaged software products are designed with business processes that can be modified by the customer. These are in the area of CRM, HRM and SCM. These applications currently have the largest market share of the SaaS market.

The companies in this packaged solution space are Netsuite who offer a global CRM, Global Accounting, ERP and Global Ecommerce solutions, business intelligence and Ecommerce solutions.

RightNow, provides a complete CRM product suite that delivers enriched sales and marketing customer experiences across multiple channels.

Constant Contact provides email marketing, event management, marketing campaign and social media productivity tools.

On the collaboration front GoogleApps boasts a user base of a 100 million business users utilising various collaborative applications.

2. Collaborative Software

This area is dominated by applications that facilitate group collaboration these are typically email, web conferencing, project management, document editing and productivity tools. Collaboration as a service is occupied by established market players and new entrants.

Microsoft Live is Microsoft's answer to conducting audio visual meetings online by using live meetings which allows you to collaborate online. Through an interface that as the same look and feel of your conventional MS Outlook user interface, with additional functionality, such as live video, audio and the ability to upload documents for meeting attendees to review, providing comments and download in real time.

Lotus Live is Lotus' bid to offer a cloud solution that provides online meeting facilities, event management, instant messaging and social networking functionality made accessible through the use of a browser.

Zoho, provides a large array of apps for productivity tasks such as presentations, hosting meetings, timesheets, word processing and project management. One of the primary benefits

is that it provides plugins to MS Office. These plugins allows users to connect to Office whilst logged into their Zoho account. This makes it more favourable than Google Docs, as documents created in Zoho are compatible with MS Office applications. The SaaS applications provide a self service interface, administrative functionality, allowing you to add and delete user permissions and access to application sets. This is how user consumption is tracked for billing and auditing.

Cloud Computing and applications delivered through the browsers removes the need to install applications locally. With the only perceivable limitation being access to the browser and prevailing internet speeds. This removes the need for future upgrades, maintenance and ongoing support of expensive applications.

(Hurwitz J, 2009), provides a description of an ecosystem as a set of partners that come together to develop applications that create value around a particular vendors product. This creates additional products that sit on the top of the infrastructure already created by the SaaS vendor. This is how SaaS vendors build their brand and power in the market place. The interoperability is facilitated through the development and use of open Application Programming Interfaces (API).

1.4.2 Infrastructure as a Service (IaaS)

IaaS shares many similarities with Internet Service Providers. In both instances they rent infrastructure for the purpose of running applications. IaaS is the delivery of computing

hardware, networks, servers and networking technology hosted within a data centre. The IaaS customer rents services instead of buying and maintaining their own infrastructure and data centre. (Turner, 2011)

IaaS is the maturity of ISP. It pools resources making it possible to respond to customer demand. Whenever you buy a service or request more capacity it is available within hours. (Hurwitz J, 2009)

Companies will usually consider IaaS based on the premise and the need to reduce start-up and ongoing operational costs. It is a given that the corresponding Service Level Agreements (SLA) change according to usage.

The most important player in the market place to date is Amazon and this was born out of their own need to increase their base infrastructure to support their online business. They soon found that their infrastructure was underused and that there was a demand based on customer infrastructure requirements. Hence, Amazon EC2, Elastic to Computing was offered as a service. This resulted in subsequent spin off services of which Amazon Simple Storage Service S3 provides storage space grouped together in different configurations.

The service in its most basic form is the rental of servers, delivered to the customer through a web service interface. Through this interface the user is able to create virtual instances of servers at the click of a button. It allows you to specify sizes and configuration. This then corresponds and translates into a recurring monthly fee. EC2 runs on Microsoft Windows Server, Linux and Sun Microsystems platforms. Hewlett Packard and IBM have developed their own cloud computing offering in this area. Amazon follows a two tier pricing model the user is charged by the data transfer rate or hourly charge for virtual machine. This is especially useful for organisations where seasonal systems peaks and troughs exist.

For example, where there is a need to increase resources for the month end reporting, development of test servers in a test environment, large volume transactions following a marketing campaign or to undertake research and development.

Based on the evidence gained from secondary based research it can be argued that the key to the use of IaaS is that companies can now have available to them powerful data centres and all the services associated. Such as access to backup, security and data management services at a fraction of the cost. The main issues with this platform are costs and security both of which vary significantly depending on vendor. (Velte & Velte, 2009) Not to mention the loss of control. In summary the main benefits of Iaas are the reduction in costs due to a reduction in IT staff, storage space and energy consumption bills.

1.4.3 Platform as a Service (PaaS)

PaaS provides a complete architecture model that delivers the application, interface development, middleware, deployment infrastructure and testing environments. It delivers a remotely hosted platform and allows the subscriber to build enterprise class applications, on demand locally for a nominal subscription fee.

It is a one stop shop for the design, application development, integration and deployment. It can even handle your storage needs. The integrated lifecycle platform provides a full development environment inclusive of collaborative tools, web interaction, programming language and operating system. It provides the complete platform for development without the expense of buying individual tools. (Turner, 2011) PaaS Storage provides an add on demand file storage and database capability whilst maintaining persistent applications. Operations take care of backup and restore ensuring application availability. PaaS in conclusion provides a well tuned stack and integrated services with access to an enterprise-class development environment.

PaaS companies often offer the following:

A workflow engine

- Development tools
- A testing environment
- An ability to integrate databases
- Third party tools and services

The characteristics of a PaaS environment are as follows;

1. It supports the development lifecycle
2. It provides a development language
3. It leverages the internet
4. PaaS platform must provide services to interfaces such as SOAP and XML
5. It can create enterprise applications by combining business logic and rules
6. Mashup's that allow two or more business services to come together and share their data
7. Portals that act as organised components bringing a suite of applications together for the service user. (Turner, 2011)

1.4.4 Security as a Service

Security as a Service is the delivery of core IT security services remotely over the internet. Traditional security has been the preserve of the internal IT department. It is typically used where there is a need to secure a cluster of cloud resources that you leverage within your enterprise. Due to the recent developments of identity management solutions it is now possible to deliver on demand encryption. As more companies store their corporate data in the cloud there will be an increase in the need for Security as a Service and the security measures that it employs. Not all companies have the inhouse skills or will want to maintain a permanent security function.

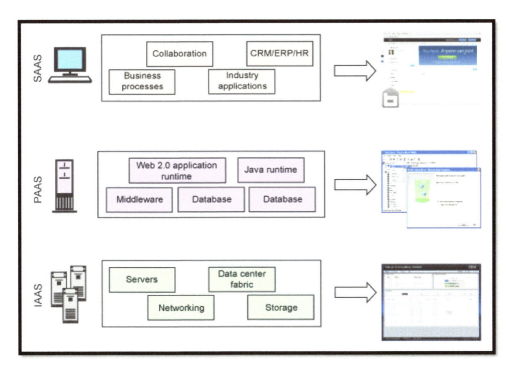

Figure 1 Layered Cloud Services

(IBM, 2010)

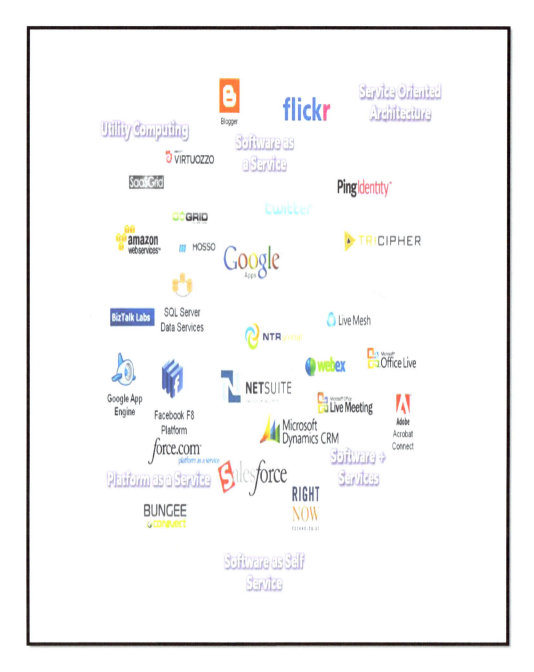

Figure 2 Cloud Services Landscape

(Sparkindark, 2010)

1.5 Cloud Deployment Models

There are four main deployment models for cloud computing these are; The **Public Cloud**, it provides a cloud infrastructure for public use and is delivered by organisations selling this as a service. The **Private Cloud** is a cloud infrastructure that is managed by a third party for the sole use of a single enterprise it can exist in one of two scenario's either on the customers site or in the providers datacentre. It is hosted behind your organisations firewall and is a more expensive solution as opposed to the public cloud. A **Community Cloud** is where a number of institutions have come together to benefit from the economies of scale resulting from shared cloud infrastructure typically used when there is a community based initiative such as a research project that have many stakeholders. It may also be managed either on or offsite. Lastly the **Hybrid Cloud** is made up of two or more cloud types either community, private and or public cloud. Each of these models support different requirements and have different constraints so you need to ensure that you choose the model that is fit for purpose and specific to the organisations needs.

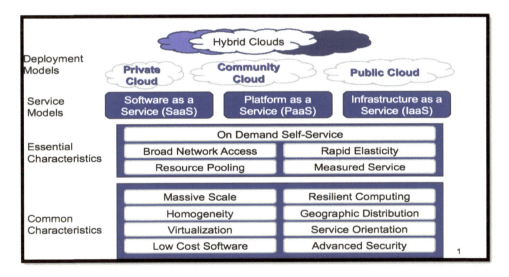

Figure 3 Cloud Computing Deployment Models

(Consulting, 2010)

There are three main roles in Cloud Computing and these are; A Consumer who consumes a service and a provider who provides a service to one or more consumers and a integrator or broker who assembles many services of various providers to offer a new service.

2.0 Chapter Two - Cloud Service Provider Focus

"As technology migrates from traditional on premise model to the new cloud model services evolve daily". (Rittinghouse, 2009)

2.1 The Google Cloud

Googles current service offerings in the SaaS market place are as follows; Gmail, Chrome browser, Android OS and Google Apps. Google Apps provides messaging and collaboration tools for Business, schools and non profit organisations. Google Apps leverages the complete suite of Google applications.

Google cloud connect for MS office is a free plugin that lets you share and simultaneously edit, MS Word, Powerpoint and XL spreadsheets. It allows you to upload and synchronize files that are stored in the cloud. This makes the files available to other users who can access the files from anywhere in the world using either a browser or mobile device. All that is required is a free plugin and a google account.

Google Sites can store a range of media resources such as videos, presentation materials, and documents in a central location. This facilitates the collaboration between local and global project teams. The advantage of this tool is its ability to accelerate the creation of secure web pages that can be used for corporate intranet or blogs without the need to understand formal programming languages such as C++ or PERL as it uses templates.

Google groups are available to business premier and education customers making it easier for users to collaborate and communicate in groups. Each group shares a common email with permissions set that defines access rights to documents, sites and calendars. IT staff are responsible for managing access rights using a secure control panel however they are no longer required to manage group creation or the addition or deletion of group members.

2.2 The Amazon Cloud

Amazon EC2 provides an elastic web service, delivered through a web interface that allows you to resize your computing estate as required. It provides the capacity to bring servers on and offline within minutes. Making it easier for systems administrators to commission or decommission servers. You only pay for your actual disc space usage. It provides developers the tools to build and test applications in discrete environments. It provides admin access and control of virtual instances. As it facilitates routine systems maintenance and remote server administration using web service API's. It also allows you to choose your own customised configuration with options to select CPU, memory and storage instance making it notionally easier to scale your enterprise.

Once you plug into the EC2 service you plug into the Amazon product suite, this includes Amazon SQS and Relational Database service. It includes its own secure interface that allows you to configure port settings on the firewall allowing you to manage controlled access to network and group instances. This feature is extremely important when running different environments on different platforms such as Linux or Windows server. This is Amazons attempt to provide a Relational Online Analytical Processing (ROLAP) solution inclusive of storage and query functionality across a range of applications. This would typically be used where you have a requirement for data warehousing.

Amazon seems to have covered all the bases in their service delivery strategy as they have in place clear guidelines well thought out data replication, storage and backup device decommissioning policies in place. This will overcome stakeholder's fears and concerns over security and what happens to your data when the service is de-commissioned.

Amazon WebServices (AWS) security features provide robust security against Distributed Denial of Service (DDoS) Attacks by ensuring the use of multiple providers for internet access. It overcomes Man in the Middle Attacks by ensuring that all API are made available via Secure Socket Layer – protected endpoints to provide server authentication. Amazon EC2 Amazon Machine Image (AMI) generates new secure host (SSH) host certificates and logs them in the management console. A customer then uses a secure API to access the host certificate before logging onto the instance.

Amazon EC2 also provides multi factor authentication to access the administrative hosts that are designed to protect the management platform. The Guest operating systems provides the customer with autonomous control over their virtual instances. The Amazon team by defacto do not have access to the Guest Operating System. This feature overcomes the concerns about company data being accessible by a third party.

The Amazon firewall comes delivered in a deny all state. This puts the responsibility on the customer to open the required ports to allow the appropriate inbound traffic. The firewall allows the traffic to be blocked by using a number of variables. This could be by service port, IP address or protocol. The firewall can be configured in groups that perform different types of functions. For example the web servers would have specific ports open to the internet either Port 80 (HTTP) or port 443 (HTTPS). The application tier of servers, open the application specific port only for the web server use. The database server in turn would open its port 8000 for communication with the application server. All three tiers of servers can only be accessed internally for systems administration on port 22 behind the corporate Firewall.

The diagram below depicts this operation.

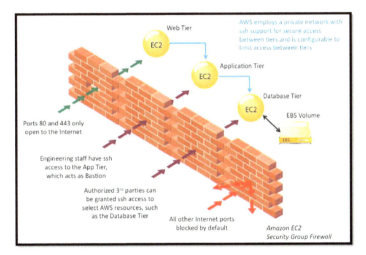

Figure 4 Amazon EC2 services being accessed behind a firewall

(Amazon, 2010)

Amazons Suite of products, Virtual Private Cloud, EC2 and S3 have achieved the Federal Information Security Management Act (FISMA) accreditation from the US General Services Administration which requires that systems controls and configurations be fully documented.

It includes the operational and technical process used to secure physical and virtual infrastructure. It provides CIO's peace of mind when considering deploying their mission critical systems into the cloud through the comfort of knowing the product as conformed to rigorous standards of operation.

2.3 The Microsoft Cloud

Office 365 professional and small business provides web enabled tools to access its established MS Office suite of products and collaboration tool (share point) on a subscription basis. Whilst Office 365 for medium sized business and enterprise service provides the online capability of its familiar suite of applications in the cloud. MS Sharepoint and Exchange Online are its product offerings.

MS Windows Azure allows developers, to build scalable applications in Microsoft datacentres without having to invest in costly hardware or having to worry about the integration of existing and new applications. It uses a Service Bus that provides secure messaging, by using communication protocols and connectivity capabilities that facilitate the building of loosely coupled services in the cloud. You only pay for the number of connections that your enterprise uses between the service bus and your applications. HTTP and REST are supported from non .NET platforms.

The benefit of Azure is that it provides the ability to setup and manage IP based network connectivity between windows azure cloud services and on premises systems. Making it easier to migrate and integrate existing applications through direct IP connectivity. MS Web server extends Microsoft's SQL server platform into the cloud. It provides automated failover and redundancy including disaster recovery of data that is geographically dispersed amongst its data centres so you would never need worry about a site being affected by natural disaster. The information below provides a comparison of return on investment and cost savings of a MS Axure's virtual server instances as opposed to an on premise configuration.

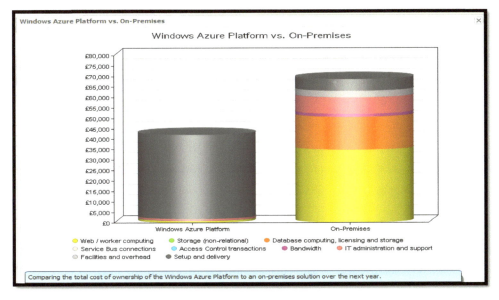

Windows Azure Platform vs. On-Premises (virtualized)			
Windows Azure Platform Savings Over One Year Analysis Period	Windows Azure Platform	On-Premises (virtualized)	Windows Azure Platform Savings vs. On-Premises
Web / worker computing	£935	£34,838	£33,903	97.3%
Storage (non-relational)	£34	£18	(£16)	-86.2%
Database computing, licensing and storage	£81	£15,759	£15,678	99.5%
Service Bus connections	£0	£0	£0	0.0%
Access Control transactions	£2	£0	(£2)	0.0%
Bandwidth	£48	£1,461	£1,413	96.7%
IT administration and support	£740	£7,942	£7,202	90.7%
Facilities and overhead	£0	£2,918	£2,918	100.0%
Setup and delivery	£40,542	£5,950	(£34,591)	-581.3%
Total Cost Over One Year Analysis Period	£42,380	£68,887	£26,507	38.5%
Number of Instances / Physical Servers	0	2		
Average Total Cost per Month	£3,531	£5,741	£2,209	
Net Present Costs (discount rate = 11.0%)	£41,950	£67,136	£25,186	37.5%

Figure 5 MS Azure Onsite Offsite Cost Comparison

(Microsoft, 2011)

Instances where MS Axure may be used are in the deployment of a fully configured development, test and production environment. Microsoft are leveraging all of their existing technology and know how to provide a premium cloud service to capitalise on their existing user base to gain market share of the PaaS market.

Salesforce delivers a CRM service and social networking capability in the cloud. The CRM portal allows you to create single views of marketing campaigns, leads and customers. It coordinates your sales and marketing efforts. By generating leads, reporting on progress and tracking the results of opportunities by using workflow and real time analytics. The Information is centralised and improves efficiency by saving time searching for information. **Chatter** is Salesforces answer to facebook and it allows you to collaborate and chat (live) to colleagues and business partners to resolve complex issues.

Service Cloud is aimed at the call centre market and allows you to connect with your customer on a variety of communication channels. It enables call centre staff to manage logged cases via a service desk. This is managed in the cloud through a variety of mediums such as Social media, email, and telephone or even on live agent web chat. It provides a real time view of service metrics of cases by agent, cases closed or cases by channel. It even allows you to view and track conversation feeds as a result of posting a blog on your companies' facebook page. The service cloud console handles cases from both traditional and modern channels. When a call comes in a screen pop ups giving you the details of the customer showing the products they purchased, cases they have logged and the service entitlement and key social sites visited. By using the video and face time feature that is available on mobile devices for example an iphone you can see what the customer sees and guide them to problem resolution. In my opinion this tool will be useful for organisations that provide IT services and support to a client base that is geographically dispersed as it would save significant time and money in travelling expenses or merely to manage a organisations sales cycle and associated activities. It could also be argued that by its very nature and inherent knowledge base, it provides call centre staff with a wealth of customer data at their finger tips. This would undoubtedly help to foster greater customer service and an enriched customer experience.

In Summary Cloud Services provide organisations with the provision of remote resources from which they can run their services or applications, which extends beyond your corporate firewall. Therefore it is imperative that you have a clear understanding of what enterprise resources exist both internally and externally to your organisation especially when considering cloud services. It is imperative to have well designed architecture, as this makes it easier to adopt new services. The benefit to this approach is that you do not have to buy additional servers and or associated infrastructure to put in your data centre or pay for expensive support staff to maintain them. The main characteristics of cloud services are scalability, low barriers to entry, low market entry costs, nominal or no capital expenditure required for infrastructure. It provides device and location independence, which allows you to access the services from virtually any access device from anywhere in the world. This is why the proposition is particularly appealing to consumers and new start ups businesses.

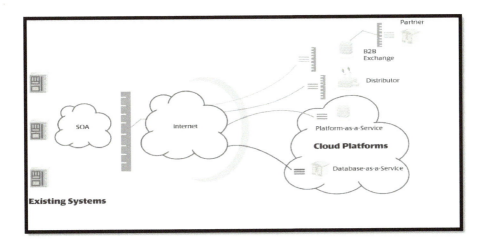

Figure 6 SOA and Cloud Service Integration

(Rittinghouse, 2009)

3.0 Chapter Three – The Underlying Technology

In this section the anatomy of the underlying technology is reviewed, to provide clarity as to whether cloud computing is a new fad without standards. Or is it a mature offering of what is currently available within the market place with the distinction that it is wrapped and packaged as a service.

Cloud computing provides services by using a combination of existing technologies. The core technologies being web services and applications. It is evident that without the advent of Web applications and Web Services SaaS and PaaS could not exist. Due to cloud services being dependent on all of the frameworks discussed within this chapter.

3.1 Service Orientated Architecture

SOA is the business and technical approach used to architect your company's business processes into reusable, interchangeable black box services. (Hurwitz J, 2009) Service orientated architecture is designed as a service that provides the ability to easily assemble and reconfigure systems in a loosely coupled architecture. It is a strategic framework of technology that allows interested systems either internal or external to the organisation to expose and access defined services and information bound to that service. (Linthicum, 2009) It consists of a set of business services that are used to realise an end to end business process. It provides added value by reducing costs, reuse of legacy systems and code whilst increasing agility. You can make changes at the configuration layer instead of re-architecting your infrastructure. It reduces the time to market for new products and services by packaging functionality of applications together. A supply chain would typically be made of interlinking systems that would involve services that check credit, inventory and shipping status. Due to SOA's modular approach, you can assemble and integrate your services to align with your business needs allowing you to easily adapt to change. In its simplest form SOA provides the user with the ability to interact via a web browser requesting information such as exchange rates. This system will then make a call to an external system, for example it could be a travel agents database to find the latest exchange rate for that day and then present that information back to the user with the current exchange rate taking care of the business logic in the background. All major vendors now support SOA solutions with the provision that the solution supports web services. Due to, "SOA being intrinsically reliant on web services"

(Erl, 2005) IT governance is an important facet of the corporate governance matrix, used to manage the control and support of IT services. Consequently, it encompasses organisational and IT support processes and as such needs executive support as it covers the complete spectrum of the organisations architecture. The Cloud computing model is supposed to extend and build on SOA requirements, such as governance, elasticity and location independence. (Halpert, 2011) However as cited, "It is a fundamental part of the architecture that has almost completely been ignored by cloud computing" (Rittinghouse, 2009)

Below is an example of the building blocks of a SOA metamodel. It shows the process/orchestration layer where you can make changes to business processes without having to change the underlying components. This epitomises a loosely coupled architecture.

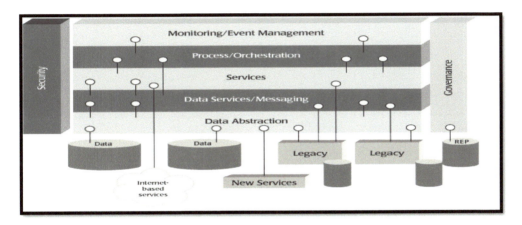

Figure 7 SOA Meta Model

(Linthicum, 2009)

When you think of the prospect of SOA and how it can leverage Cloud Computing you can consider it as a major value proposition for an enterprise that requires the benefits that both technologies provide.

In summary SOA is an architectural paradigm for managing processes of new and existing heterogeneous systems that are under the control of different organisations. It fosters interoperability and loose coupling of services and systems. Whilst complimenting Cloud computing by allowing you to access cloud services outside of the corporate firewall as if it were another service contained within the SOA. It requires an end to end appreciation of your architecture as well as tightly administered policies, processes, contracts and service level agreements. The differentiator between SOA and Cloud Services is that SOA delivers web services to other programs and cloud computing delivers software services to consumers. SOA is therefore an essential enabler to cloud computing as it provides the mechanism by which IT infrastructures can be connected to a shared pool of resources to deliver IT services. These are accessed via virtual machines and external services through the cloud.

This makes it easier to transition from a SOA to a cloud environment. The following is an example of SOA leveraging Cloud Services as if it were another service contained within the SOA.

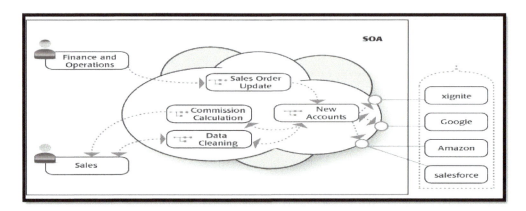

Figure 8 SOA interfacing with Cloud Services

(Velte & Velte, 2009)

3.2. Web Services (WS*)

Web Services refer to a collection of standards that address interoperability. These standards not only define the format of the interfaces used to specify service contracts and services they also define the protocols used to communicate. There are numerous web services that are grouped under the following specification types; Metadata, Reliability, Security, Transaction, interoperability and resource specifications. In this review we will review a small sample of those available.

Web Services provide a standard using Simple Object Access Protocol (SOAP) to integrate web based applications. SOAP messages are encoded as Extensible Markup Language (XML) documents that support interoperability between different systems. The SOAP Message consists of an envelope, a header that is optional and a body that is mandatory.

Its primary function is to invoke remote procedural calls to remote systems. This is where it provides business value as it provides the framework for connection of remote clients. This allows developers to write code in the form of triggers to interrogate a data base and extract the relevant data that is fed back to the requester in a presentable format.

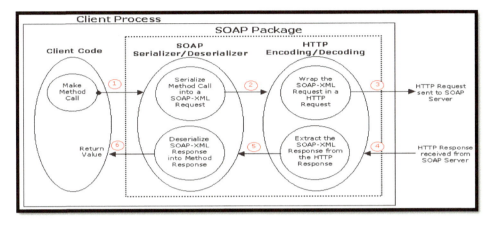

Figure 9 SOAP Message Request/Response

(SoapUser.com, 2009)

The Web Services facilitates the communication between different applications that originate from different sources by using what is known as an Extensible Markup Language document (XML). XML is a meta language that encodes documents into machine readable formats. The WSDL defines the XML based protocol that is used to define the web service contract. It specifies the location of the web service, the operation it exposes, the SOAP message involved and the communication protocol that talks to the service. The constructed service should be registered with the Access Control List along with the needed guidelines and Meta data information in a reachable service registry. It allows all partners in the service to find them. The UDDI is one of the most popular examples available for service registration platforms in the market. This is due to it being a standard that major manufactures endorse and its simplistic registration process for services. SOA and Web Services are an important part of the cloud computing model because both approaches place a priority on understanding the business needs and delivering services that add value as the business needs change.

It is unknown to the majority of users that cloud computing leverages the already existing web service protocols as ratified by World Wide Web Consortium (W3C). W3C are responsible for ensuring compatibility and standardisation for the World Wide Web. Below is an example of the SOAP/XML message process.

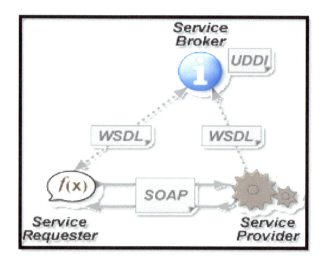

Figure 10 XML Message Exchange

(Velte & Velte, 2009)

- WSDL describes the service
- SOAP is the XML based protocol that provides the messaging format between Service Requester and Provider
- UDDI provides the service registry format

The following are web service extensions that are typically used when using web services with a Service Orientated Architecture (SOA).

3.2.1 WS Reliable Messaging (WSRM)

The reliable messaging delivery standard defines a messaging protocol to ensure the reliable delivery of messages by identifying, managing and tracking messages during communications. It integrates with WS security and WS policy. It specifies the SOAP bindings necessary for interoperability. The wire protocol includes specific header and message detail between sender and receiver. The quality of service defines the operations (Submit, Notify, Deliver, Respond) between service providers and users. It is the execution of a transport-agnostic, SOAP-based protocol providing quality of service in the reliable delivery of messages. (Iwasa, 2004) So by using WSRM you can be rest assured that messages are sent and received securely by using the web services suite of protocols.

3.2.2 WS Security

WS Security is used to build secure web services to implement message maintaining confidentiality and integrity. It is flexible by design and supports the Secure Socket Layer, Kerbros and PKI's. It supports multiple security tokens, electronic signatures and multiple encryption technologies. It defines the security related data that is required in the header element of Simple Object Access Protocol message. It specifies how security information is presented within the SOAP message. As SOAP messages can be exchanged using different protocols such as Websphere, SMTP and HTTP The main feature of WS Security is that it maintains message confidentially, integrity and delivers security tokens. By itself it does not provide a robust security framework. However by leveraging web services and higher level application specific protocols you can accommodate a large number of security configurations and technologies. (Nadalin, 2004)

3.2.3 WS Policy

The WS Policy has policy-aware tools that understand policy expression and responds appropriately. Policy refers to an information set known has a policy assertion. This expression is an XML representation of the policy and it is the XML that facilitates the interoperability between different platforms.

In summary web services have become the de facto standard for SOA and is based on core protocols such as WSDL, HTTP and XML. (Josuttis, 2007)

3.3 Security Assertion Markup Language (SAML)

SAML is based on an XML framework used for sharing user authentication, entitlement and attribute information between web services it is the glue that enables the loose coupling of services.

The SAML SSO provides a single log-on which is authenticated by an identity provider who then enables you to access other systems/services that is entrusted as a gatekeeper. This is why it is the key to the loose coupling of services. It is responsible for the exchange, authorisation and authentication details by sharing security tokens between different security domains, organisations and applications. It is a flexible standard that supports Single Sign On (SSO) with multiple partners. It controls the access to resources by authenticating users without storing passwords, as the applications that use SAML accept secure tokens. This provides a substitute for multiple passwords. SAML performs two fundamental functions, making decisions about access control based on policies and enforcing the decisions. Below is an example of a SSO.

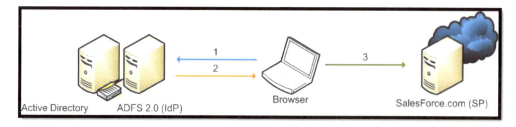

(Goodwin, 2011)

1. User authenticates to security server requesting sign on to SalesForce Server
2. The security server then passes a SAML assertion back to the browser
3. Automatically the browser submits the assertion (token) to SalesForce server that logs in user.

SAML is made up of the following components;

Assertion and protocol: This manages the request and response protocols, semantics and syntax when defining code assertions.

Bindings and Profiles: Maps the SAML request/response message exchange into lower level communications protocols such as SOAP and or SMTP. A profile is the set of rules that govern how the information is extracted from the lower communications layer.

Conformance Specifications: Sets the basic standards to which the SAML specification must conform.

Security and privacy considerations: This covers the risks that SAML is exposed to and how they are mitigated.

In summary the advantage for SAML is as follows; Platform Neutrality, as the security framework is independent of the architecture, loose coupling of directories, user information does not have to be maintained across multiple directories. It improves the online experience by facilitating single sign on, users sign only once and are then authenticated to other service providers. Whilst reducing costs, improving security and increasing productivity. Its importance and relevance is captured in the following statement.

"Those that have gone through the pain of supporting multiple proprietary SSO implementations are now mandating the use of SAML for internet SSO with SaaS applications and or other external providers." (Identity, 2011)

4.0 Chapter Four – Key Governance Frameworks and Controls

4.1 Importance of Corporate Governance and IT Governance

Corporate Governance is the broad term that refers to the rules, processes and procedures that governs how a business, enterprise and even countries are operated, regulated and controlled. It provides guidelines and a set of responsibilities that should be exercised by the board and executives to ensure company objectives are achieved. Whilst ascertaining the risk and managing them appropriately. It maintains the integrity of the organisation and verifies that resources are used responsibly. To afford a degree of protection to the organisation, customers, suppliers and stakeholders (Grant, 2010)

Within the Governance framework, IT governance is an important component, even more so in today's competitive market place. IT Governance is "*a framework for the leadership, organizational structures and business processes, standards and compliance to these standards, which ensure that the organization's IT supports and enables the achievement of its strategies and objective*". (Calder, 2007) From this statement it can be seen that, IT governance is a fundamental requirement in an enterprises toolboxl as it seeks to understand the strategic importance of IT in helping the organisation to achieve its corporate objectives whilst mitigating all risks and issues as appropriate. It is about understanding the IT related risk the business is exposed to. It guides and informs IT strategy and plans whilst directing the use of IT resources to minimise risk, maximise profit to build current and future value.

In the 21st century computing, software applications and systems are at the heart of business operations and this is why Governance, even more so IT governance at both the strategic and operational levels are areas of concern. Especially in light of WorldCom and Enron scandal (SearchCIO, 2004) that centred on accounting irregularities that sparked international focus. The Sarbanes-Oxley Act 2002 was legislated. It included internal control assessment and corporate governance. This suggests that there is a prevailing issue that needs to be addressed by a sustained approach from management to implement and support the required frameworks and controls. Ensuring that policies are communicated and translate to controls at the operational level to enforce good governance. As it has been found that IT controls have been traditionally lax according to Rittenhouse governance has been overlooked. No wonder it has been notorious for attracting the attention of auditors. Some organisations have outdated and untested system operational procedures. Or just a lack of knowledge of the scope and depth of the controls that are required. These controls within the context of IT governance are COBIT, ITIL, ISO27001 and Prince 2.

4.1.1 Service Governance

Service governance as related to cloud services comes into its own with cloud computing. As it is used to manage the systems leveraged and cloud policies in an enterprise architecture. It manages auditing, event logging, service validation that determines how to maintain service levels, online upgrades, and versioning. In short it ensures the service is doing what it is supposed to do.

Design time service governance provides a run time integrated repository that manages the service from development to deployment. It monitors and manages the services whilst they are being executed. Equally important are the people who will be responsible for implementing processes and service governance. It is also important for the people responsible for the strategic direction, the build, the control and monitoring of cloud computing systems. To be involved in the implementation of the governance model or else you will have difficulty in making it succeed. Therefore it is vitally important to gain all stakeholder participation and buy in into the process.

4.1.2 Why IT Governance is important?

All businesses use IT in varying degrees to support their business initiatives. It is important that IT and risk associated with key internal business functions are governed and managed according to the needs of the business. By implementing and maintaining a robust IT governance process you can control business risk, provide increased infrastructure and internal service levels whilst improving operational efficiency. It empowers IT managers to correlate relationships between IT systems and business risks so that the technology risk can be understood from a business perspective. Due to the visibility of the IT infrastructure it enables decision makers to make decisions with clarity of how to best optimize performance whilst minimising business risk and exposure. This is how IT becomes a strategic enabler to the organisation. This is of particular relevance when you consider that due to the nature of business today many organisation generate revenue from ecommerce websites and as such unscheduled downtime can negatively impact on a company's reputation, market value and share price. Too often organisations are found to have out dated processes and procedures that are not dynamically linked to other parts of the IT system and thus unable to show and demonstrate impact of failure, which leads to weaknesses and gaps in terms of reliability and availability. Therefore an IT governance solution allows organisations to more effectively manage risk whilst being able to track, monitor and report on key performance indicators for IT projects.

The use of KPI's within the context of IT helps organisations to measure the value of IT projects relative to a benchmark that has been set. This in turn enables you to calculate Return on Investment (ROI). (Hardy, 2006) argued that "organizations need a strong governance model in place to approve, prioritize and manage IT investments on an ongoing basis. This is necessary to align IT investments with the business requirements needed to deliver IT value to an organization". (Linthicum, 2009) Stated that "*there is little notion of governance today within cloud computing, and thus there is little control and implementation of policies. Therefore, many enterprises are not diving right into the cloud*". I wonder if this is the reason why uptake has been slower than expected amongst some organisations despite the obvious advantages. This then creates a massive opportunity to develop a governance framework toolkit to manage a systematic and controlled migration to the cloud.

To develop a robust governance model as applicable to cloud computing there are a series of preliminary steps you have to take and they as follows;

- Identify key stakeholders
- Select Governance Board
- Identification of Critical Success Factors
  - Mandate from executive endorsing governance structure
  - Clear understanding of objectives and outcomes
  - Change management, ensuring changes as a result of new governance models to be communicated consistently
  - Customisation of governance model as appropriate to meet the needs of the organisation
  - Quick win, the implementation of activities that can be implemented swiftly and provide immediate results

4.2.4 Weigh up the Risks – Risk Management

Risk is a natural part of the business landscape. If left unmanaged, the uncertainty can spread like weeds. If managed effectively, losses can be avoided and benefits obtained. (ISACA, 2010)

Figure 13 Risk Management Process

(Jasny, 2008)

It is prudent that the IT Department perform risk assessment to determine the impact and cost of their potential cloud service becoming unavailable for any stated period of time and what is viewed as acceptable outages. (Halpert, 2011) provides a useful cloud risks and mitigations matrix. This should then translate into SLA's that the Cloud service provider will honour. It would appear that cloud providers limit the amount that they have to pay out in the event of a severe outage to the yearly software contract fee. (Grobauer, 2011) In his recent article on the vulnerabilities of cloud computing cited, *"that cloud computing core technologies web applications, services and cryptography have vulnerabilities whether that be due to it being state of art implementations or intrinsic to their existing technology platforms. He further describes examples such as session riding, hijacking, virtual machine scape, DOS attacks and obsolete cryptography that represent threats from using virtual machines and browser technology"*. He further elaborated and gave a practical example of categorizing the types of vulnerabilities that are intrinsic to cloud services. The vulnerabilities he cited are as follows;

Unauthorised access to the management console which is particularly high due to the way the services are delivered.

Internet protocol vulnerabilities, due to how the cloud is accessed across networks this can make it especially susceptible to man in the middle attacks. Data Recovery vulnerabilities where computing resources are expanded and contracted this gives rise to the reuse of pooled resources making it possible to recover data written by previous user.

Metering and billing evasion is where a bill can be manipulated and or avoided.

Poor key management procedures, cloud computing infrastructure are required to manage and store many different keys. The difficulty lies in being able to apply a common standard that can be used across cloud infrastructures.

(Grobauer, 2011) comments further on to say that "*currently there are no standardized cloud-specific security metrics*" and that until such time that it may be near impossible to assess and audit security in a cloud environment. I do not agree with this point of view. I would view Cloud technology as a process of leveraging existing technology and standards. This being the case, one can create a benchmark for operation within existing frameworks by integrating the likes of COBIT, ITIL, and PRINCE2 in a governance light model. In his paper (Abu-Musa, 2007) cites that " *the outcome of a survey that was undertaken was that, where there is an increased use of IT controls, it correlates with higher performance across a range of operations, audit, performance and security. The direct correlation between performance measures and activities demonstrates that the implementation of COBIT best practise framework improves an organisations performance*".

Note that different service providers will provide different levels of security protection as applicable to the particular service and in most cases they will provide more security than that is readily available to small organisation such as SAS 70, SSL and two step authentications which provides a first tier of security. It is also pertinent to find out from the service providers how they propose to mitigate the identified risks. How are system outages communicated and what the response procedure is, how it is invoked and how the customer's response team is notified? And what is considered to be a service outage. These are fundamental questions and you need to have a communication plan that identifies key contacts whilst integrating the service seamlessly with your internal support mechanisms. The limitation of this research is such that I was not able to implement a large scale cloud service therefore I was unable to test the service provider's claims that they publish in their normal marketing publications.

However it should be noted that when a cloud provider delivers cloud services across international boundaries then the country where the service is provided and data resides has jurisdiction over that data meaning that the personal data will be subject to that countries laws pertaining to data protection. It is imperative that you have a clear understanding of the data protection laws in the country where you propose to store your data. You also need to know what happens to your data after the contract has ended and stipulate timeframes for the return of your data. A Chinese proverb states "the bigger the risk the bigger the reward" (Turner, 2011). The following diagram depicts the devolution of systems control as you move from on premise systems to cloud services.

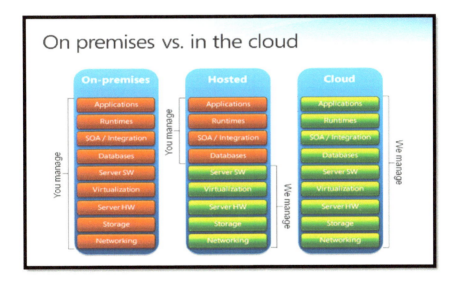

Figure 144 On Premise vs Cloud Service Apex of control

(Save9, 2010)

ITIL is a best practise framework that defines the role of IT Service management. It gives direction of how to best use IT resources by documenting the functions and processes to achieve business value. This approach consists of two complementary processes, service delivery and service support.

With five main objectives;

- Alignment of IT with current and future needs;
- Tune Capacity and scalability of IT Services;
- Reduce costs and of process and procedure development;
- Increase throughput and optimisation;
- Improvement of IT service delivered

The UK Office of Government (OGC) summarise the role of ITIL, "*The focus of ITIL today is integration of IT into the business, assuring the delivery of business value and the treatment of services as business assets*" (Gateway, 2011).

A service level is the cornerstone of every IT service delivered into an enterprise. (Carl, 2011) It is an agreement between a provider and its customer. As it specifies the service to be provided, the timeframe and how it will be measured. It defines the agreed service between two parties and sets out the remedial action and or penalties that are imposed if the service falls below a particular threshold. They are supposed to formally document business requirements instead of solely being a tool used to invoke penalty payments or service credits. A comprehensive service level agreement will typically include some or all of the following sections within the agreement;

- Contract
- Amendments
- Service Description
- Service Availability
- Service Hours
- Reliability
- Customer Support
- Service Performance

Functionality

- Change Management Procedure
- IT Service Continuity
- Security
- Printing
- Charging (if applicable)
- Service Reviews
- Glossary
- Amendment Sheet

(Transfer, 2007)

In Chapter 1, we explored the cloud computing paradigm and how the technology has evolved, the business drivers involved, globalization and the increasing need for business' to collaborate and become efficient in the 21st century to ensure survival. This is why this paradigm shift is significant and relevant to how society consumes services both now and in the near future.

With the development of the internet and networking technologies the infrastructure that hosts a myriad of different services has taken second place to the services. Applications offered on that infrastructure. The providers of such services the likes of Amazon, Microsoft and IBM have changed their business models by providing remotely managed services that allows the use of pooled resources/virtual servers that are used by multiple consumers delivered at a lower cost. It facilitates ease of market entry. In essence it is what we have already experienced with companies hiring rack space for their own hardware in a data centre. The only real difference being deployment methods as it is easier to commission and decommission virtual servers delivered through your browser in this new landscape. Another example is in the case of SaaS implementations, as it is cheaper to deploy and maintain than the traditional on premise model for example the reducing the need to renew expensive licensed software. The main drivers for business decisions today being; cost, performance, and increased productivity. Along with the advent of the internet and what subsequently followed IP telephony the costs for communications had receded making it a more cost effective proposition for corporates to become global. It facilitated the provision of media rich content including video, text and voice. Collaboration has helped to increase productivity by reducing the distance between space and time allowing people to contribute from anywhere in the world as long as they have access to an internet browser, this facilitated global collaboration. Both Google and Facebook are at the leading edge in the development of collaboration tools. It is a given that collaboration supports business and lends itself to doing things better. To realise these benefits the organisational culture must be one that fosters collaboration and as such business processes must be developed to embody good IT governance whilst leveraging cloud services that overcomes time and space. The current economic climate is raising concerns for business' who are required to maintain share price and keep employee moral high whilst increasing productivity. Companies are now seeking to provide better levels of service to maintain customers and look for innovative ways to work with new and existing partners to provide new business models. It is impossible to outguess the market so it makes perfect sense to select a technology partner that goes through a 3 – 6 month development cycle enhancing existing products. To ensure organisations stay abreast of technological developments.

In my opinion cloud computing will revolutionise the world of computing and how we access services in the present and near future, as it leverages established technologies such as the internet, SOA and Webservices to deliver cloud services in its current form.

It was found that each of the cloud service offerings although they may be distinctly different shared the same fundamental characteristics. Such as low initial investment, (you pay per usage) rapid elasticity, pooled resources and advanced security. As well as significant reductions in Capex and Opex costs.

An ideal would be for governments to leverage these services making savings on their total IT expenditure and then these funds could be redistributed to alleviate poverty. It has such a far reaching impact. The US government are seeking to harness this technology at the time of writing. It can also be used to supplement an enterprises DR strategy by providing remotely distributed architecture. This can be an alternative to a hotsite that may only be accessed from specific locations and requires dedicated connectivity. Traditionally most IT companies govern the five technology layers within the enterprise however as they move from IaaS, PaaS to SaaS that control is transferred to the cloud service provider. As the diagram below depicts the locus of control moves towards service provider depending on the service you adopt.

On Premise	On Premise (hosted)	IaaS	PaaS	SaaS
App	App	App	App	App
VM	VM	VM	Services	Services
Server	Server	Server	Server	Server
Storage	Storage	Storage	Storage	Storage
Network	Network	Network	Network	Network

Enterprise has control	Enterprise shares control with vendor	Vendor has control

Figure 15 Loss of Control Matrix

(Guo, 2010)

Despite the obvious advantages there is still apprehension at the prospect of moving core services to the cloud as organisations are concerned about the security of data, authentication, data disposal, performance and loss of control of their systems. As moving to the cloud irrespective of service offerings brings new issues such as;

- Service interruption
- Vendor Lock in
- Vendor viability
- Portability issues across cloud providers

To this end we reviewed the main players in the cloud computing space by services offered. It was found that companies were stampeding to enter this new market with me too products as there are low barriers to entry. However the companies who had the greatest market share were already tried and tested brands such as Amazon with their EC2, IaaS solution, Microsoft with their PaaS solution, Microsoft Azure and Google with their SaaS solution Google Apps and how they worked. It was found that they had developed mature product offerings and enviable support infrastructures that their consumers could benefit from immediately. In the case of Amazon they have a very mature service offering which has fulfilled regulatory requirements and recently been accredited by FISMA.

Whilst companies need to maximise the added value that cloud computing presents they need to do so in a way that limits their exposure to the inherent risks that are associated with losing control of their systems and data. This can only be achieved by the implementation of management policies, processes and audit procedures that underpin the implementation and delivery of the service on a daily basis. (Guo, 2010)

The argument for cloud always "starts with efficiency" but should quickly focus on quality of service and IT agility, said EMC's Mirchandani. Mark Egan of VMware considers three distinct phases that I would argue are useful to begin to shape the direction and growth of an organisation. The first being an awareness of cost savings, the business impact, the types of risks involved and a appreciation of what governance should be in place. The second phase being the migration of mission critical applications and finally the third phase focuses on agility. (Tucci, 2011). In my opinion it would be prudent to have a firm understanding of what the cloud service will provide you at each of the corresponding phases. Whilst being objective and realistic in your evaluation of the level of your organisations technological maturity. So that you can readily determine what parts of your IT function can be safely and securely migrated to the cloud.

An assumption was made that the underlying technology was developed and already existed and was in fact a predecessor of cloud computing. It was found that the underlying technology and control frameworks have been established and being used in industry for the last decade. What the subsequent grounded research provided was the evidence that proved the assumption to be correct, as we explored.

In the research undertaken to develop Chapter 3.0 conclusive evidence was provided through the exploration of the fundamental building blocks that are used to build Cloud Services. In particular the Service Orientated Architecture (SOA) which provided the architectural design principle as well as the platform that facilitates the interoperability between different services. We found that Web Services provide the standards and protocols by which the different applications/services communicated. Both of these frameworks are mature in their own right and are being widely used in industry. This was an important finding because it means that what we currently see in the form of cloud services is actually the maturity of SOA, and it is these frameworks and standards that are used to underpin cloud services.

However this still was not the full story as there is still concern from companies around governance and controls as discussed. We know that once a company moves their IT function into the cloud they lose control as shown in the cloud service adoption model matrix. (Fig 16) Therefore it is important to understand governance and the controls that are at your disposal. As there is a presumption that there are no standards or metrics available to measure cloud services.

In Chapter 4.0 we reviewed governance and it was found that governance subsumed IT governance and that at a macro level governance provided the framework for the executive board to guide the organisation strategically. Whilst at the micro level IT governance translated into policies and procedures that governed how IT is used and the tools that are employed to help achieve the business objectives. We saw that through the adoption of IT governance processes, policies and procedures. The enterprise has a means by which to gather metrics on performance and ROI, if implemented effectively it can help organisations become more efficient in the process. However pivotal to the success is the involvement of all key stakeholders to enforce policy consistently across the enterprise. *"No large scale or business critical project should ever be managed on a standalone basis. The need to involve and secure buy-in from functions right across the organisation means that a project governance approach is essential. While project management is the key discipline within this, project governance is broader in scope and has six interlinked objectives:*

1. Ensuring real business value through project and business alignment.

2. Controlling costs through centralisation.

3. Maximising resource allocation, particularly of high value resources.

4. Risk management through portfolio balancing.

5. Uniform application of best practice.

6. Organisational coherence" (Calder, 2009)

So why is governance in the cloud such a hot topic and cause for concern? In particular the area of service management which focuses on security, availability and liability. The wiki leaks fiasco exposed the risk to cloud computing and resulted in a subsequent distributed denial of service attacks. For this very reason it is important to have Service Level Agreement in place. (Turner, 2011)

Cloud computing governance should cover all aspects of cloud services. It should define, track and monitor the execution of services regardless of the platform or type of cloud service. (Linthicum, 2009) A good place to start is in the area of service governance as these policies will detail the service location, dependency and service security. When applying security it is advised to apply the appropriate system level access controls. Before embarking on this process of developing a service governance model you need to be clear about what you propose to govern.

(Hurwitz J, 2009) Has provided a useful list of what to consider below;

- Who can access the service
- What they can do to the service.
- How changes to the service affect other services.
- How changes to the service affect applications.
- How governance works with security.
- How governance links into service testing.
- How governance works with service delivery.
- How to set and maintain appropriate service levels

According to (Kandukari, 2009) if governance is properly administered it will cover the following issues that may arise;

- It identifies and define the customer's needs
- It provides a framework for understanding
- It simplifies complex issues
- It reduces areas of conflict
- It encourages dialog in the event of disputes

It is of paramount importance for companies to employ robust IT governance and security frameworks, such as ITIL, COBIT and ISO 27001 as they are proven globally recognised standards that are designed help manage and control the use of IT resources effectively. This I would suggest is a prerequisite before an organisation can realise the benefits of the cloud computing.

 The main features that are sought by companies embarking on a cloud strategy are;

1. Security
2. Transparent controls (User interface)
3. Systems operating at specified (SLA's) (Turner, 2011)

The cloud is built using existing technology however it's the service portion that is what is intangible in the equation. With liability still a very real issue. (Smith, 2010) Observed that even though there is great promise with cloud computing there are also inherent risks. For example Cloud providers will only payout to the value of lost service time and not to the value of loss of business. This would suggest that at a micro level this is an area that requires close attention in contract negotiation and at a macro level for insurance companies to provide adequate cover for loss of revenue.

I would consider Cloud computing as an appropriate technology for an organisation when the data in that organisation does not have a high security rating such as restricted or classified. Where the organisations architecture is well documented, and architected to be able to leverage cloud services easily, or where your organisation is at the desired level of maturity to be able to leverage the services safely. It is also well suited to Greenfield site scenarios where the main objective is collaboration, cost reduction and the use of the internet browser is the desired platform of choice.

Conversely it would follow that cloud computing is not appropriate if your systems are tightly coupled. Or where the inhouse interfaces are poorly designed and when you cannot risk losing control of mission critical applications and or operations. Whilst cloud computing may be an evolutionary step to deliver and receive services, it is of vital importance that you understand the solutions and the resources that are available in the market place. Businesses who aspire for best practise must have a robust management framework and toolsets that are to be consistently applied to ensure a successful outcome when using IT to support strategic objectives. (OGC, 2008)

When considering a provider it should be considered from the point of view of what controls they employ as we discovered there are various control frameworks that can be deployed to establish good practise and good governance. We explored the COBIT, ISO 27001, ITIL and Prince 2 controls that provide a complete suite of standards that regulates the use and management of IT systems. At the operational level there are a number of tools at your disposal these come in the form of Web Services that provide the standards to govern the reliability and security of data in flight whereas the KMIP, SAML/SSO ensure secure exchange of encryption keys and single sign on to systems. It was found that both COBIT and ITIL can readily be customised to map to cloud deployments. Whilst Prince 2 is a project management methodology that lays a heavy emphasis on managing risk and delivering projects in a controlled environment. In effect the same rules of engagement apply in the cloud as it would in on the premise systems when it comes to security. However you need to understand the system boundaries and apply the security procedures and policies that provide a secure, reliable and efficient IT provision. This I would suggest would take the form of a matrix, whereby you tailor the application of policies and procedures as appropriate to fulfil the organisations legal and regulatory requirements.

Cloud computing is not the elixir for all computing scenarios and as such it would be to your organisations detriment to think it is. However it does provides great potential and scope for an IT manager seeking to reduce Capex costs and ensuring that they have a stake in the future. It promises to shape our futures and as such every discerning CIO, IT Manager and or technologists should look at the opportunity to see what Cloud Computing as it can be concluded that it is a well established technology and deserves its place in within a companies IT strategy. It will impact every sphere of our lives and how we receive essential services.

6.0 Chapter Six - Recommendation

To be able to determine if cloud computing is the right platform for your organisation there are quality questions that you must ask, with the basis of the question being. What is it that you and your organisation are trying to achieve and what resources you will use to get there? (Johnson & Scholes, 1998) define strategy *"as the direction and the scope of the organisation over the long term that achieves the advantage for the organisation through the configuration of resources within a challenging environment in order to meet the needs of the market and fulfil stakeholder expectations"*. By undertaking strategic analysis it provides an organisation with a framework for asking the tough questions of which (PESTLE) analysis is an easy framework to work with and will allow you to quickly identify key areas both internally and external to your organisation and the environment it operates within. This information can then be used to guide strategic decisions.

(Velte & Velte, 2009) state, when considering cloud computing as a solution you should at the outset be clear on the your corporate IT structure, how much capacity you will use, the regulations governing your data, speed of delivery and cost benefit/ratio.

Cloud computing may not be appropriate for your organisation and it could be for a number of reasons. Ranging from size of the organisation, restrictive regulatory requirements on data or not deriving any financial benefit from moving to a Cloud service.

These are the instances that I suggest you would use cloud computing, when you are required to evaluate or stress test new software application in isolation. The same applies for systems integration test where you are likely to require additional resources for a short period of time, therefore it will be more cost effective to achieve the desired result through PaaS. I would also suggest that you use IaaS to cope with seasonal peaks in your workload thus removing the need to buy the extra capacity to cope with the peaks and troughs that may be a result of either month end or year end reporting requirements.

From a tactical point of view when considering cloud services yes it is an attractive proposition from the onset, lower Capex, lower total cost of ownership and scalable resources. However you should also think of the long terms costs associated. In the case of a PaaS environment other costs may be introduced at a later stage for ongoing support and development.

In theory the cloud vendor will have its own backup strategy that the company buys into however the company needs to know to what extent the data is backed up. As it may not be sufficient for your requirements or what is required with reference to your IT governance protocols. The disaster recovery and business continuity plans should also consider scenarios where the provider's service or third party service is not available. It is recommended to have fully documented and tested workarounds that should be tested in conjunction with the service provider.

It is also pragmatic to find out what your data centre costs are. What are the costs of each application? So you can determine if your data centre has future capacity based on growth forecasts. Or whether to migrate noncore services to the cloud.

A word of caution would be to understand the legal requirements on data retention as different countries will have different privacy and confidentiality laws. For example in the UK Health Level 7 sets standards for the transfer of medical information between systems. In the future they may start to impose fines like their US counterparts, so ensure that before you place data in the cloud you know under whose jurisdiction your data falls under and who regulates it. In some countries penalties could be a fine or even a custodial sentence. The following table shows the level of fines imposed for not adhering to legal requirements and regulations in the US.

	Sarbanes-Oxley	Fair and Accurate Credit Transactions Act of 2003 (FACTA)	HIPAA
Directors and Officers	$1,000,000		
Institution	$5,000,000	$11,000	$50,000 to $250,000
Prison	20 years		1 to 10 years

Figure 16 Fines Imposed for Breech of Confidential Data Laws in the US

(Velte & Velte, 2009)

It is therefore imperative to ensure that the cloud service provider fulfils the following obligations;

- Preserves authentic and reliable data including metafiles and log files
- Ensure the data is secure and protected
- Provides clear guidance on where the data is to be hosted especially in compliance with local laws
- Service provider to allow access to systems to monitor performance or test for vulnerabilities known as a right to audit clause that may be necessary to satisfy statutory regulation.

If you have specific hardware needs and or need absolute control of your server and confidential data then it would not be feasible to store this data offsite. Where you have two applications that you need to integrate it is prudent for them to co-exist in the same location to overcome network latency, security and reliability. Where you run applications internally and it is dependent on external data from the cloud, your application will only run as fast as the cloud service provider will allow. Therefore at the architectural design stage you should clearly map your data sources and locate them for optimum system performance and data retrieval. If latency is a concern then the cloud may not be a viable option. It is recommended that in this scenario it would be advisable to run the application and data sources locally until you can host the complete infrastructure in the cloud.

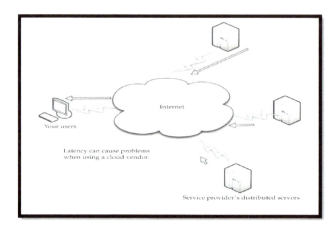

Figure 177 Latency in the Cloud

(Velte & Velte, 2009)

Some applications may not be ready for the cloud and may not communicate securely across the internet therefore you will need to ensure that it is compatible with proprietary web browsers and able to communicate securely using SSL Encryption. Where security and privacy of your data is paramount you can encrypt the data before you store it on the vendors cloud. So if someone does access your data they will not be able to read it. SAML with SSO with also provide an extra layer of security for single sign on to cloud services.

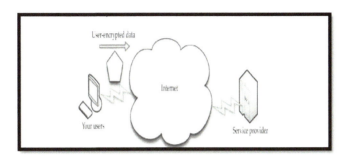

Figure 18 User Encrypted Data

(Velte & Velte, 2009)

It is imperative that you work out the figures. What will it cost to buy the required hardware and to pay the support staff to run it? If after comparison the figures are less than what it would cost to go to the cloud then you would be advised to stay with a conventional computing setup.

(Escalante, 2011) Provides a practical initial first series of assessment questions in understanding how your service provider delivers its service. It is vital to obtain an answer or see documentary evidence during the service provider assessment process:

- A clear undertaking by the provider as to what they consider as a service outage
- Evidence of how they ensure confidentiality and the integrity of data hosted.
- Provide evidence of having achieved the BCP standards BS 25999
- How they provide protocols for the commission and decommission of services
- Documentation of the providers risk assessment protocols
- How does the service provider process the data or do they store the data?
- Is the data stored on campus in a datacentre or in the cloud?
- Do service providers pass data to third parties?

- Is the data encrypted when it is in transit or at REST
- Are Service Provider backup's stored offsite?
- Once data is destroyed is it done in such a way the data is unrecoverable?
- Review of the providers ability to deliver a service that conforms to legal and regulatory frameworks both in the country of operation and globally. If you are negotiating with a service provider for Private Cloud managed services. To ensure that your organisation is not exposed it is advisable to have your legal team review the terms of agreement so that you understand what both you and the service provider is liable for. From a technical point of view it is also prudent for security personal to be involved in the development of SLA's to ensure that security requirements are contractually enforceable. It also makes sense to establish operational metrics before you move to the cloud, this will establish a baseline to measure if there is a degradation of service. It is therefore recommended to re-evaluate your risk tolerance thresholds in light of the information you receive from your provider. This should be included your risk management plan but must also includes elements of the service providers risk plan. It must include details that cover availability, service outage, business continuity and disaster recovery.

Other related work cited by (Guo, 2010) confers that cloud computing" needs governance". And that a well defined cloud computing governance model is a prerequisite to successfully implement cloud computing. I concur with this point of view and recommend that the following frameworks and controls be applied to your organisation. Its level of application will be specific to the size of your organisation. It can also be applied irrespective of the type of cloud service adopted in order to achieve organisational and management objectives.

These are as follows;

- **Governance procedures and processes** to manage the on-premise and cloud-based services, encompassing the management and policies implemented across the enterprise.
- **Management of Resources**; processes that are used to manage cloud-based services throughout its lifecycle
- **Service management**; looks at the cloud as a reliable resource and addresses liability cover, who is responsible when an unscheduled service outage occurs.

- **Compliance management**; to perform impact analysis on new regulations, provision of compliance reporting and notification of breeches.
- **Policy management**; to be able to monitor and manage policies supporting compliance initiatives including the provision of reports on activity
- **Policy schemes** and templates that protect manage and monitor cloud-based services.
- **Services profiles** and policy schemes that includes core infrastructure, platforms and software configurations
- **Risk management;** identify, track and report on risk management activities

Consumers of cloud services must ensure that they perform the appropriate due diligence on cloud service providers to be sure of their capability. Where there is overlap in terms of the application of governance processes between consumer and provider then these should be included as part of the risk assessment and included in service agreements as appropriate. This means that you will have to incorporate a robust risk management methodology from the outset.

If a company spends the time to evaluate cloud computing and cloud provider capabilities and put in place the appropriate IT governance frameworks to offset risk then a company may be able to realise the promise of Cloud Computing in the 21st century.

References and Bibliography

Abu-Musa, A. (2007). *Exploring COBIT Processes for ITG in Saudi Organisations: An Empirical Study.* Egypt: Tanta University .

Alliance, C. S. (2011, August 26). *Cloud Control Matrix (CCM).* Retrieved September 7, 2011, from Cloud Security Alliance.org: https://cloudsecurityalliance.org/research/initiatives/ccm/

Andries. (2006). Adaptation in new technology-based ventures:insights at the company level. *International Journal of Management Reviews Vol 8 No. 2* , 91 - 112.

Bakker. (2008). Putting e-commerce adoption in a supply chain context. *International Journal of Operations & Production Management Vol. 28* , 313-30.

Bernstein, D. (2010). Intercloud Security Considerations. *2nd IEEE International Conference on Cloud Computing Technology and Science* (p. 539). IEEE Computer Society.

Brooks, C. (2011, September 14). *Harvard University Preps for Cloud Move.* Retrieved September Thursday, 2011, from SearchCloudComputing.com: http://searchcloudcomputing.techtarget.com/news/2240084575/Harvard-University-preps-for-cloud-move

Buckley. (2011, July 22). *Fierce Telecom.* Retrieved September Thursday, 2011, from Fierce Telecom: http://www.fiercetelecom.com/story/cloud-computing-can-reduce-business-energy-costs-123b-says-att-verdantix-st/2011-07-22

Calder, A. (2009, June 3). Retrieved July 23, 2011, from http://www.articlesphere.com/Article/IT-Project-Governance-And-Prince2-Project-Management--How-To-Keep-Major-IT-Investments-On-The-Rails/33621?&lang=en_us&output=json&session-id=d5916e483cca43334fcd229ce54dba18

Calder, A. (2009, January). Retrieved September Friday, 2011, from http://www.projectsmart.co.uk/project-governance-prince2-project-management.html

Calder, A. (2007). *IT Governance: A Pocket Guide.* Cambridge: IT Governance.

Carl, B. (2011, June 1). *Cloud SLA's the next bugbear for Enterprise IT.* Retrieved September Friday, 2011, from SearchCloud Computing.com: http://searchcloudcomputing.techtarget.com/news/2240036361/Cloud-SLAs-the-next-bugbear-for-enterprise-IT?asrc=EM_EDA_14018952

Chaganti, P. (2008). Cloud computing with Amazon Web Services. *Developer Works* .

Chan. (2002). Management and business issues for B2B eCommerce implementation. *Proceedings of the 35th Hawaii International Conference on System Sciences - 2002* (pp. 5-7). Hawaii: IEEE Computer Society.

Consulting, I. C. (2010, June 1). *Cloud Computing FAQ.* Retrieved August 10, 2011, from IT Cloud Consulting: http://www.itcloudconsulting.com/cloud-computing-faq/

De Silva, N. (2010). Cloud Computing - A Driving Platform for Business Strategies. *Developer Works* .

Department for Business Innovation And Skills. (2009). *Digital Britain.* London: Crown.

Doom, C. (2009). Criticial Success factors for ERP implementations in Belgian SMEs. 2-3.

Dure'ndez, L. &. (2007). Managerial behaviour of small and medium sized family businesses:an empirical study. *International Journal of Entrepreneurial Behaviour & Research Vol. 13 No. 3* , 151 - 72.

Erl, Thomas. (2005). *Service-Oriented Architecture: Concepts, Technology, and Design.* London: Prentice Hall.

Escalante, E. A. (2011, July/August). EDUCAUSE Review Magazine Volume 46, Number 4, July/August 2011. *Policy Matters (Campus Environment & Political Context)* .

Essex, D. (2006, April 24). *Washington Post Newsweek Interactive*. Retrieved July 20, 2011, from Washington Technology: https://submit.ac.uk/viewGale.asp?oid=40226199&key=6cf89cbbf15c2b61839c61bd6c3aa78e&lang =en_us&output=json&session-id=d5916e483cca43334fcd229ce54dba18

FGI. (2009). *Prince 2* . Retrieved July 3, 2011, from FGI Training and Consultancy: http://www.fgiltd.co.uk/frequently-asked-questions/prince2/

Gateway, O. (2011). Service Level Agreements. *IT Governance* .

Goodwin, R. (2011, July 30). *SalesForce SSO with ADFS 2.0 – Everything you need to Know*. Retrieved August 5, 2011, from Rhys Goodwin Weblog: http://blog.rhysgoodwin.com/cloud/salesforce-sso-with-adfs-2-0-everything-you-need-to-know/

Granovetter. (1985). Economic action and social structure:the problem of embeddedness. *The American Journal of Sociology Vol.91 No 3* , 481 - 510.

Grant, K. (2010). *Strategic Information Systems Management.* London: Course Technology.

Grobauer, e. a. (2011, MARCH/APRIL). Understanding Cloud Computing Vulnerabilities. *IEEE Security & Privacy* , p. 52.

Guo, Z. (2010). *A Governance Model for Cloud Computing.* Beijing: School of Computer, Beijing University of Posts and Telecommunications.

Hall. (2001). Entrepreneurship as radical change in the family business:exploring the role of cultural patterns. *Family Business Review* , 193 - 208.

Halpert, B. (2011). *Auditing Cloud Computing.* United States: Wiley Corporate F&A.

Hardy, G. (2006). *Using IT Governance and COBIT to deliver value with IT and respond to legal, regulatory and compliance challenges.* Egypt: Information Security Technical Report .

Hurwitz J, e. a. (2009). *Cloud Computing for Dummies.* Wiley.

IBM. (2010, December 7). *Cloud and Industry PAAS Best Practice and Patterns*. Retrieved September 17, 2011, from developer works: http://www.ibm.com/developerworks/cloud/library/cl-cloudindustry1/

Identity, P. (2011, March). *SAML Tutorial*. Retrieved September Thursday, 2011, from pingidentity : https://www.pingidentity.com/resource-center/SAML-Tutorials-and-Resources.cfm

IEC. (2008, June). ISO38500 ISO 38500 IT Governance Standard. *ISO38500 ISO 38500 IT Governance Standard* . London, UK: IEC.

ISACA. (2010, January). *Risk IT*. Retrieved September Friday, 2011, from ISACA.org: http://www.isaca.org/Knowledge-Center/Risk-IT-IT-Risk-Management/Pages/Risk-IT1.aspx

Iwasa, K. (2004). Web Services Reliable Messaging TC WS-Reliability 1.1. *OASIS Standard* , 4.

Jarillo. (1989). Entrepreneurship and growth:the strategic use of external resources. *Journal of Business Venturing Vol. 4 No 2* , 133 - 47.

Johnson, G., & Scholes, K. (1998). *Exploring Corporate Strategy*. London: Prentice Hall.

Josuttis, N. (2007). *SOA in Practice.* Sebastopol: O'Reilly Media Inc.

Kandukari, R. B. (2009). Cloud Security Issues. *IEEE InternationalConference on Services Computing* (p. 2). Pune, India: Advance Software Technologies International Institute of Computing.

Kessinger, K., & Duffer, J. (2008, June 21). *COBIT Fact Sheet*. Retrieved July 12, 2011, from isaca.org: http://www.isaca.org/About-ISACA/Press-room/Pages/COBIT-Fact-Sheet.aspx?&lang=en_us&output=json&session-id=d5916e483cca43334fcd229ce54dba18

Lanz. (2002). Worst Information Technology Practices in Small to mid size organisations. *The CPA journal* , 71 - 74.

Linthicum, D. S. (2009). *Cloud Computing and SOA convergence in Your Enterprise.* Chicago: Addison-Wesley Professional.

Lukhele, S. (2011, September 21). NDISA SaaS Implementation. (B. Turner, Interviewer)

Marasini. (2008). Assessment of e-business adoption in SMEs: A study of manufacturing indusrty in the Uk North East region. *Journal of manufacturing Technology Management Vol. 19 Iss:5, pp.627 - 644* , 11.

Miller, M. P. (2008). *Cloud Computing: Web-Based Applications That Change the Way you Work and Collaborate Online.* London: Que.

Misra, S., & Monal, A. (2011). Identification of a Company's suitability for the adoption of cloud computing and modelling its corresponding Return on Investment. *Telecommunications Software Engineering: Emerging Methods, Models and Tools* , 504-521.

Nadalin, A. (2004, February 1). Web Services Security. *OASIS Wen Services Security:SOAP Message Security 1.1* .

Nah. (2001). Critical Factors for Successful integration of enterprise systems. *Business Management Journal Vol. 7 No. 3* , 285-96.

OASIS. (2009). *Key Management Interoperability Protocol (KMIP).* United Kingdom: OASIS.

OECD. (2004). *ICT, Ebusiness and SME's.*

OGC. (2011, January). Retrieved September Thursday, 2011, from IT Governance: http://www.itgovernance.co.uk/sla.aspx

OGC. (2008). Aligning COBIT 4.1, ITIL V3 and ISO/IEC 27002 for Business Benefit. LONDON: OGC.

O'Neill, Martin. (2009, April 27). Connecting to the cloud, Part 1: Leverage the cloud in applications.

Pettey, C. (2006, October 8-13). *http://www.gartner.com/it/page.jsp?id=496886*. Retrieved September Monday, 2011, from Gartner Newsroom: http://www.crmlandmark.com/saasmarket.htm

Rittinghouse, J. W. (2009). *Cloud Computing: Implementation, Management, and Security.* United States: CRC Press.

Save9. (2010, March 5). *Business & Internet - Cloud Solutions.* Retrieved July 7, 2011, from Save9: http://www.save9.com/cloud-computing/custom-cloud-solutions/

SearchCIO. (2004, June 7). *CIO Sucker Punch in SOX.* Retrieved August 11, 2011, from media.techtarget.com: http://media.techtarget.com/searchCIO/downloads/TheCIO_SuckerPunch_in_SOX.pdf?&lang=en_us&output=json&session-id=d5916e483cca43334fcd229ce54dba18

Smith, & Thong. (2007). An integrated model of information systems adoption in small businesses. *Journal of Management Information Systems* , 187 - 214.

Smith, L. (2010). Public Cloud Computing Risks must be overcome as part of the IT Strategy. *SearchCIO.com* .

SoapUser.com. (2009, September 10). *SOAP Basics.* Retrieved September 15, 2011, from Soapuser.com: http://www.soapuser.com/basics4.html

Son, S., & Weitzel, T. e. (2005). Framework for IT Performance Management Systems. *The Electronic Journal Information Systems Evaluation* , 219-228.

Sparkindark. (2010). *www.sparkindark.com*. Retrieved September 16, 2011, from www.sparkindark: www.sparkindark.com/wp-content/uploads/2011/09/sparkindark_cloudcomputing.png

Sultan, N. (2010). Cloud Computing for Education: A New Dawn. *International Journal of Information Management 30* , p. 110.

Surya, B. (2011, January 25). *Where Is Cloud Computing Going? Up, Up and Away.* Retrieved September Tuesday, 2011, from Cloud Tweaks Plugging into the Cloud: http://www.cloudtweaks.com/2011/01/where-is-cloud-computing-going-up-up-and-away/

Teo. (2004). Adopters and non-adopters of business to business electronic commerce in Singapore. *Information and Management* , 89 - 102.

Transfer, K. (2007, January 31). *Service Level Agreement*. Retrieved June 20, 2011, from Knowledge Transfer.net: http://www.knowledgetransfer.net/dictionary/ITIL/en/Service_Level_4

Tree, L. (2011, July). *Agile Cloud Computing*. Retrieved September Thursday, 2011, from Perspectives on Cloud Computing : http://cloud-computing.learningtree.com/2011/07/06/%E2%80%9Cagile%E2%80%9D-cloud-computing/

Tucci, L. (2011, May). *http://searchcio.techtarget.com/tip/CIOs-dissect-evolving-role-of-the-CIO-in-cloud-and-mobile-computing?asrc=EM_NLT_13939907&track=NL-983&ad=834310HOUSE&*. Retrieved September 23, 2011, from SearchCIO.com: http://searchcio.techtarget.com/tip/CIOs-dissect-evolving-role-of-the-CIO-in-cloud-and-mobile-computing?asrc=EM_NLT_13939907&track=NL-983&ad=834310HOUSE&

Turner, B. (2011). *Research Proposal: Cloud Computing and Corporate Governance: Is the technology mature enough for companies to incorporate into their Corporate IT strategy.* London.

Tyler. (2007). Services business markets:a further view of a new reality or blurred landscape? *Journal of Services Marketing Vol. 21 No. 5* , 295 - 303.

Velte, T., & Velte, A. (2009). *Cloud Computing a Practical Approach.* Vancouver: McGraw Hill.

West. (2010, April). Saving Money Through the Cloud. p. 4.

Winans, et al. (2010). *Cloud Computing - A collection of working papers.* London: Deloitte Consulting.

www.ingramcontent.com/pod-product-compliance
Lightning Source LLC
LaVergne TN
LVHW012315070326

832902LV00001BA/18